Hungry Girl

HAPPY HOUR

Also by Lisa Lillien

Hungry Girl:
Recipes and Survival Strategies
for Guilt-Free Eating in the Real World

Hungry Girl 200 Under 200:
200 Recipes Under 200 Calories

Hungry Girl 1-2-3:
The Easiest, Most Delicious, Guilt-Free
Recipes on the Planet

Hungry Girl Chew the Right Thing:
Supreme Makeovers for 50 Foods You Crave
(recipe cards)

Hungry Girl: The Official Survival Guides:
Tips & Tricks for Guilt-Free Eating
(audio book)

Hungry Girl

HAPPY HOUR

75 Recipes for Amazingly Fantastic Guilt-Free Cocktails and Party Foods

Lisa Lillien

St. Martin's Griffin
New York

HUNGRY GIRL HAPPY HOUR: 75 RECIPES FOR AMAZINGLY FANTASTIC GUILT-FREE COCKTAILS AND PARTY FOODS. Copyright © 2010 by Hungry Girl, Inc. All rights reserved. Printed in the United States of America. For information, address St. Martin's Press, 175 Fifth Avenue, New York, N.Y. 10010.

www.stmartins.com

Cover design and book design by Elizabeth Hodson

Illustrations by Jack Pullan

Food styling and photography by General Mills Photography Studios

Additional food styling and photography by Kelly Cline

ISBN 978-0-312-62103-2

First Edition: June 2010

10 9 8 7 6 5 4 3 2 1

This book is dedicated to
all of the fun-loving HG fans
who can drink legally and
choose to drink responsibly.
Designated drivers ROCK.

Contents

Chilly Chocolate Mudslide
Frozen Fudge–Dipped Strawberry Mudslide
Spiked Pumpkin–licious Nog

Acknowledgments

Since this book is itty-bitty, I'm not going to do the usual long-winded thank-you thing. I'd like to thank the HG staffers, who work incredibly hard, day in and day out, to make Hungry Girl the best brand (and most enjoyable place to be!) in the universe:

Jamie Goldberg
Alison Kreuch
Lynn Bettencourt
Lisa Friedman
Dana DeRuyck
Callie Pegadiotes
Lisa Foiles
Adam Feinsilver
John Vaccaro
Elizabeth Hodson

The following people also deserve credit, and I happen to enjoy them immensely. In alphabetical order:

Jeff Becker, Nanci Dixon and the General Mills photography crew, Jen Enderlin, Tom Fineman, John Karle, Neeti Madan, John Murphy, Val Pensky, Jack Pullan, Matthew Shear, Bill Stankey, Gary Stromberg, and Anne Marie Tallberg.

And also to:

My amazing husband, Daniel Schneider; my wonderful parents, Florence and Maurice Lillien; Meri Lillien; Jay Lillien; the entire Lillien and Schneider families; and to all of the HG subscribers.

Bottoms up!

Introduction

Welcome to *Hungry Girl Happy Hour*, the cutest cocktail book in the universe! On these pages you'll find recipes for 50 amazingly delicious, completely guilt-free cocktails and 25 incredible HG-friendly party foods. These drinks and snack foods are SO fantastic, no one would EVER believe they're low in calories and fat. NO ONE. Not your skeptical nosy neighbor. Not your diet-food-hating best friend. Not even your beer-guzzling husband. So quit procrastinating and start flipping through this book. Like, NOW.

<u>Things to Have on Hand</u>

There's no fancy-schmancy stuff required. Here's a list of simple things you should keep around . . .

A variety of glasses.

A few martini glasses (small and large), several tall and short glasses, a couple of shot glasses, and some margarita glasses will keep you covered.

A shaker.

Aside from helping to chill your drinks, shakers are FUN. Plus, most standard shakers include a strainer—two tools in one!

A blender.

There's a whole chapter about blended drinks. To enjoy these, you'll definitely need a blender.

Measuring cups and spoons.

Your basic kitchen tools will do. (See Handy-Dandy Conversion Chart.) But if you're feeling fancy, invest in a jigger and a spouted measuring cup with markings for each fluid ounce.

A muddler and a corkscrew.

You'll only need these for a handful of recipes. But they're worth having around.

Nonessentials for added enjoyment.

Colorful bendy straws, little paper umbrellas, toothpicks shaped like swords, a tip jar (you never know) . . . These will WOW your friends when they come over for drinks!

Things to Know

Look for rum, vodka, and tequila with 40% alcohol content (80 proof). This will ensure that your drinks taste delicious and that the nutritional info is 100% accurate.

Whenever possible, keep your cocktail ingredients cold. This way, your drinks won't be warm or watered down.

You can de-booze most of these drinks by swapping out the liquor for something else. When it comes to soda-based drinks, use an equal amount of extra soda in place of the alcohol. For creamy drinks, use more of the creamy liquid base (usually light soymilk).

Like most cocktail recipes, ours list liquid ingredients by the fluid ounce. But if you're working with measuring cups and spoons, this should help . . .

Handy-Dandy Conversion Chart

1 ounce = 2 tablespoons
2 ounces = ¼ cup
8 ounces = 1 cup

And if you're working with a shot glass or a jigger, know that 1 shot is the equivalent of 1½ ounces or 3 tablespoons.

Recommended Products

Sugar-Free Calorie-Free Flavored Syrup

Torani Sugar Free

HG Heads Up! Look for Torani at specialty stores like BevMo! and Cost Plus World Market, or order online at torani.com. Some of the more common flavors—like vanilla—can be found at supermarkets in the coffee aisle. You can also find many flavors of sugar-free syrup at some coffee chains—just ask for a few ounces of the syrup to go!

25-Calorie Packets Diet Hot Cocoa Mix

Swiss Miss Diet, Nestlé Fat Free

No-Calorie Sweetener Packets

Splenda

HG Heads Up! As far as taste is concerned, Splenda is BY FAR our favorite. However, if you prefer an all-natural option, stevia will work, too.

Light Vanilla Soymilk

8th Continent Light, Silk Light

*HG Alternative! Although technically not soymilk, Blue Diamond Unsweetened
Vanilla Almond Breeze is an amazing milk swap with only 40 calories per cup.
Use this stuff and your cocktails will have even fewer calories. Find it with
the non-refrigerated boxed milks at select supermarkets and health food stores.*

Diet Cranberry Juice Drink

Ocean Spray Diet

Diet Lemon-Lime Soda

Sprite Zero

Sugar-Free Powdered Drink Mix

Crystal Light

Fat–Free Vanilla Ice Cream

Breyers Smooth & Dreamy Fat Free

HG Alternative! Dreyer's/Edy's Slow Churned Light Ice Cream may not be fat-free, but it tastes FANTASTIC and won't affect recipe nutritionals very much at all.

One last thing:

Please, please, please drink responsibly. (That includes being of the legal drinking age.) Just 'cuz you're drinking guilt–free cocktails doesn't mean you won't be guilty of doing something TERRIBLE if you drink and drive. So be safe, okay?

That's it . . . COCKTAIL TIME!

Chapter One

Martinis & Mixed Sips

OMG! Key lime pie, Creamsicles, pumpkin-liciousness, and fruity fun.

The drinks in this chapter are almost too delicious for words. And here's a little tip: Chill out! To make your cocktails stay cold longer, stick the glasses in the freezer for a while before whipping up your drinks. Or simply fill the glasses with ice (crushed works best), and let 'em chill while you make the cocktails. COOL. Okay, let's not waste any more time. Let the mixing begin!

Kickin' Key Lime Pie Martini

PER SERVING (entire recipe, 1 martini): 129 calories, 0g fat, 21mg sodium, 7g carbs, 0g fiber, 4g sugars, 0g protein

Ingredients

1½ ounces lime vodka
1 ounce sugar-free calorie-free
    vanilla-flavored syrup
1 ounce pineapple juice
½ ounce lime juice
1 tablespoon Cool Whip Free, thawed
Optional garnish: lime slice

O For a pic of this recipe, see the photo insert. Yay!

Directions

Combine all ingredients in a glass and stir until smooth. Transfer to a shaker filled with ice.

Shake thoroughly and then strain into a large martini glass. If you like, finish it off with a slice of lime on the rim of the glass. Enjoy!

MAKES 1 SERVING

For more recipes, tips & tricks, food finds, and MORE, sign up for FREE daily emails at hungry-girl.com!

Mounds Bar Martinis

Ingredients

One 25-calorie packet diet hot cocoa mix
3 ounces vodka
2 ounces sugar-free calorie-free coconut-flavored syrup
2 tablespoons Fat Free Reddi-wip

Directions

Combine cocoa mix with 2 ounces hot water in a glass and stir to dissolve. Add 2 ounces cold water and all other ingredients. Stir until smooth.

Transfer mixture to a shaker filled with ice. Shake, shake, shake, and then strain into two martini glasses. Enjoy!

MAKES 2 SERVINGS

Mango Mmmm-tini

Ingredients

1½ ounces sugar-free calorie-free mango-flavored syrup
1½ ounces vodka
½ ounce fresh lemon juice
Optional garnish: mango slice

Directions

Pour all ingredients into a shaker filled with ice. Add 1½ ounces water and shake well.

Strain into a martini glass and, if you like, garnish with a mango slice!

MAKES 1 SERVING

Winter Wonderland Peppermintini

PER SERVING (entire recipe, 1 martini): 125 calories, 1.5g fat, 10mg sodium, 3g carbs, 0g fiber, 0g sugars, 0g protein

Ingredients

2 teaspoons Coffee-mate Sugar Free
    French Vanilla powdered creamer
1 no-calorie sweetener packet
1½ ounces vodka
¼ teaspoon peppermint extract
Optional garnish: small candy cane

 For a pic of this recipe, see the photo insert. Yay!

Directions

In a glass, combine powdered creamer and sweetener with 1 ounce warm water. Stir to dissolve. Add 1 ounce cold water.

Add creamer mixture, vodka, and extract to a shaker filled with ice. Shake well and then strain into a martini glass. If you like, garnish with a candy cane leaning jauntily on the rim!

MAKES 1 SERVING

For Weight Watchers *POINTS*® values and photos of all the recipes in this book, check out hungry-girl.com/book.

Orange Creamsicle Martini

PER SERVING (entire recipe, 1 martini): 109 calories, 0g fat, 69mg sodium, 2.5g carbs, 0g fiber, 0.5g sugars, 0g protein

Ingredients

1½ ounces orange vodka
1½ ounces sugar-free calorie-free vanilla-flavored syrup
1 tablespoon Cool Whip Free, thawed
4 ounces diet orange soda

Directions

In a glass, combine vodka, syrup, and Cool Whip Free. Stir until smooth. Transfer to a shaker filled with ice.

Add soda to the shaker and stir (don't shake!). Strain into a large martini glass and enjoy!

MAKES 1 SERVING

Java-tini

●□■□■□●□■□■□■□●□■□■□●□■□●□■□■●

PER SERVING (entire recipe, 1 martini): 123 calories, 0.5g fat, 38mg sodium, 3.5g carbs, 0g fiber, 1g sugars, 1.5g protein

Ingredients

1 teaspoon instant coffee granules
2 ounces light vanilla soymilk
1½ ounces vanilla vodka
1 ounce sugar-free calorie-free vanilla-flavored syrup
2 teaspoons fat-free non-dairy liquid creamer

Directions

Combine coffee granules with 1 ounce warm water in a glass and stir to dissolve. Add all other ingredients.

Transfer to a shaker filled with ice. Shake well and strain into a large martini glass. Sip happily!

MAKES 1 SERVING

Pumpkin Pie-tini

Ingredients

4 ounces light vanilla soymilk
1½ ounces vanilla vodka
1 ounce sugar-free calorie-free vanilla-flavored syrup
2 tablespoons canned pure pumpkin
¼ teaspoon pumpkin pie spice

Directions

Combine all ingredients in a glass and stir until smooth. Transfer to a shaker filled with ice.

Shake thoroughly and then strain into a large martini glass. Enjoy!

MAKES 1 SERVING

Light & Stormy

PER SERVING (entire recipe, 1 drink): 101 calories, 0g fat, 50mg sodium, 2g carbs, 0g fiber, 2g sugars, 0g protein

Ingredients

6 ounces diet ginger ale
1½ ounces dark spiced rum
Optional garnish: lime slice

Directions

Combine ginger ale and rum, and serve over ice. If you like, place a slice of lime on the rim of the glass. Easy and delicious!

MAKES 1 SERVING

Pink Drink

PER SERVING (entire recipe, 1 drink): 110 calories, 0g fat, 42mg sodium, 14.5g carbs, 0g fiber, 14.5g sugars, 0g protein

Ingredients

3 ounces light ruby red grapefruit juice drink
3 ounces club soda
1½ ounces passion fruit rum
Optional garnish: maraschino cherry

Directions

Combine all ingredients and serve over ice.
If you like, add a maraschino cherry to bob
around in the glass!

MAKES 1 SERVING

Spiked Almond Joy Hot Cocoa

> **PER SERVING** (entire recipe, 1 drink): 125 calories, 0g fat, 140mg sodium, 10g carbs, 1g fiber, 8g sugars, 1.5g protein

Ingredients

One 25-calorie packet diet hot cocoa mix
1½ ounces coconut rum
1 drop almond extract
Optional topping: Fat Free Reddi-wip

Directions

In your favorite mug, combine cocoa mix with 6 ounces hot water and stir to dissolve. Add rum and extract. (Remember, just one DROP of extract!)

Stir and, if you like, top with a generous squirt of Reddi-wip. Enjoy, preferably wrapped in a blanket by a roaring fire!

MAKES 1 SERVING

Peppy Cola

Ingredients

1 lime, cut into 4 wedges
5 ounces diet cherry cola
1½ ounces vodka

Directions

Over a strainer, squeeze juice from 3 lime wedges into a glass. Fill glass halfway with ice. Add soda and vodka, and give it a good stir. Plop remaining lime wedge into the glass and enjoy!

MAKES 1 SERVING

For more recipes, tips & tricks, food finds, and MORE, sign up for FREE daily emails at hungry-girl.com!

Rockin' Root Beer Float Cocktail

> PER SERVING (entire recipe, 1 drink): 98 calories, 0g fat, 80mg sodium, 0g carbs, 0g fiber, 0g sugars, 0g protein

Ingredients

4 ounces diet root beer
1½ ounces vanilla vodka
1 ounce sugar-free calorie-free vanilla-flavored syrup

Directions

Combine all ingredients and serve over ice. Tada!

MAKES 1 SERVING

Berry-licious Lemon Drop

PER SERVING (entire recipe, 1 drink): 113 calories, 0g fat, 38mg sodium, 3g carbs, 0.5g fiber, 1g sugars, <0.5g protein

Ingredients

2 strawberries, thawed from frozen
Half a 2-serving packet (about ½ teaspoon)
    sugar-free lemonade powdered drink mix
1½ ounces vodka
½ ounce lemon juice

Directions

On a small plate, mash strawberries with a fork. Set aside.

Combine powdered drink mix with 3 ounces water in a glass and stir to dissolve. Transfer to a shaker filled with ice.

Add mashed strawberries, vodka, and lemon juice to the shaker. Shake vigorously and strain into the glass. (If berries get stuck in the strainer, simply remove them and continue straining.) Enjoy!

MAKES 1 SERVING

HG Tip!

Frozen berries work perfectly here because they're typically very ripe and juicy once thawed. So if you want to use fresh berries, make sure they're extra-juicy!

Chapter Two

Margaritamania

Who needs high-calorie margaritas when you can have THESE?

Each of the 'ritas in this chapter have less than 150 calories. Shocking, but true. Oooh, here's a margarita tip: Want to give your margarita glass a fancy salted or sugary rim? Do this BEFORE you fill the glass. Pour a nice amount of salt or sweetener onto a small plate, and shake gently so that it evenly coats the bottom of the plate. Then, using your fingers, rub a little lime juice around the top edge of the glass. Flip the glass over onto the plate, wiggle it around, and turn it upright. NOW fill the glass! (FYI, using sugar won't add too many calories to your drink. We estimate you'll use about a 16-calorie teaspoon or so of sugar to rim that glass. Want to avoid sugar calories? Use Splenda!) Alright, time to make some margaritas. Pssst ... Make 'em virgin-style for the designated driver!

HG's Magical Low-Calorie Margarita

Ingredients

 For a pic of this recipe, see the photo insert. Yay!

1½ ounces tequila
1 ounce lime juice
One 2-serving packet (about 1 teaspoon)
    sugar-free lemonade powdered drink mix
6 ounces diet lemon-lime soda
Optional garnish: lime slice

Directions

Combine tequila, lime juice, and powdered drink mix in a glass. Stir to dissolve drink mix.

Add soda and stir, stir, stir. Pour into a margarita glass with lots of crushed ice. If you like, finish it off with a slice of lime on the rim of the glass. Time to enjoy!

MAKES 1 SERVING

HG Alternative!

For a frozen version, toss your mixture into a blender instead of a shaker. Add 1 cup crushed ice or 5 to 8 ice cubes, and blend at high speed until mixed well!

CONTENT 750 ML

TEQUILA

08177800

Freezy-Fresa
Strawberry Margarita

□▪

PER SERVING (entire recipe, 1 margarita): 125 calories, 0g fat,
24mg sodium, 7g carbs, 1g fiber, 2g sugars, 0g protein

Ingredients

Half a 2-serving packet (about ½ teaspoon) sugar-free
    strawberry powdered drink mix
6 ounces diet lemon-lime soda
1½ ounces tequila
4 frozen unsweetened strawberries
1 ounce lime juice
1 cup crushed ice *or* 5 to 8 ice cubes
Optional garnish: lime slice

Directions

Combine powdered drink mix with soda in a glass and stir to dissolve.
Transfer to a blender.

Add all other ingredients to the blender, and blend at high speed until uniform and slushy.

Pour into a nice margarita glass and, if you like, garnish with a slice of lime. Drink up!

MAKES 1 SERVING

HG Tip!

Feel free to experiment with whatever strawberry-blend drink mixes you find on shelves. Strawberry kiwi, strawberry banana, strawberry tangerine . . .

Cran-tastic Margarita

PER SERVING (entire recipe, 1 margarita): 108 calories, 0g fat, 40mg sodium, 3g carbs, 0g fiber, 2g sugars, 0g protein

Ingredients

6 ounces diet cranberry juice drink
1½ ounces tequila
½ ounce lime juice
1 no-calorie sweetener packet
Optional garnish: lime slice

Directions

Mix ingredients well and serve over ice. If you like, garnish with a lime slice. Yum!

MAKES 1 SERVING

HG Alternative!

For a frozen version, toss your mixture into a blender instead of a shaker. Add 1 cup crushed ice *or* 5 to 8 ice cubes, and blend at high speed until mixed well!

Mixed Berry Margarita

PER SERVING (entire recipe, 1 margarita): 146 calories, 0g fat, 12mg sodium, 12g carbs, 2.5g fiber, 6g sugars, 0g protein

Ingredients

For a pic of this recipe, see the photo insert. Yay!

½ cup frozen mixed unsweetened berries, slightly thawed
2 ounces diet lemon–lime soda
1½ ounces tequila
1 ounce lime juice
2 no-calorie sweetener packets
¾ cup crushed ice *or* 4 to 6 ice cubes
Optional garnish: lime slice

Directions

Place all ingredients in a blender, and blend until smooth.

Garnish with a lime slice, if you like. Pour, sip, and enjoy!

MAKES 1 SERVING

Razzy 'Rita

PER SERVING (entire recipe, 1 margarita): 105 calories, 0g fat, 5mg sodium, 2g carbs, 0g fiber, 0.5g sugars, 0g protein

Ingredients

1½ ounces tequila
1 ounce lime juice
Half a 2-serving packet (about ½ teaspoon) sugar-free
    raspberry powdered drink mix
Optional garnish: lime slice

Directions

Combine all ingredients in a glass with 5 ounces water. Stir to dissolve drink mix.

Transfer to a shaker filled with ice and shake it like you mean it. Pour into a glass, slap a lime slice on the rim, if you like, and enjoy!

MAKES 1 SERVING

HG Alternative!

For a frozen Razzy 'Rita, toss your mixture into a blender instead of a shaker. Add 1 cup crushed ice or 5 to 8 ice cubes, and blend at high speed until mixed well!

Chapter Three

Fun with Blenders

Blended drinks are more fun when they're made RIGHT.

We're sticklers, so read closely. CLOSER. Okay, back off, your nose is touching the page. You'll need the following:

* A good blender. DO NOT attempt to make these with a lame blender. Just don't.

* Good ice. No freezer burn allowed. No exceptions, no excuses.

* Bendy straws and cute glasses. Buy some.

One more thing . . . Crushed ice RULES. Not only is it easier to blend, but non-blended drinks full of chopped cubes are fantastic, too. Don't have a fancy fridge that spits out the pulverized stuff? Throw some ice into a sealable bag, and use a meat mallet or heavy can to smash your ice cubes. Just be careful not to beat up your countertop.

Spiked Strawberry Shake

□■□■□■□■□■□■□■□■□■□■□■□■□■□■□■□■

PER SERVING (entire recipe, 1 shake): 204 calories, 2.5g fat,
80mg sodium, 18g carbs, 2g fiber, 8g sugars, 3g protein

Ingredients

2 teaspoons Coffee-mate Sugar Free French Vanilla
    powdered creamer
⅔ cup frozen unsweetened strawberries
    (about 8 berries), slightly thawed
4 ounces light vanilla soymilk
1½ ounces vanilla vodka
1 ounce sugar-free calorie-free strawberry-flavored syrup
3 no-calorie sweetener packets
⅔ cup crushed ice or 3 to 5 ice cubes
2 tablespoons Fat Free Reddi-wip

Directions

Dissolve creamer in 1 ounce warm water.

Place creamer mixture and all ingredients except Reddi-wip in a blender. Blend at high speed until smooth.

Pour into a glass and top with Reddi-wip. Enjoy!

MAKES 1 SERVING

For Weight Watchers *POINTS*®
values and photos of all the
recipes in this book, check out
hungry-girl.com/book.

Peachy Cream Dream

PER SERVING (entire recipe, 1 drink): 179 calories, 0.5g fat, 60mg sodium, 17g carbs, 1.75g fiber, 9.5g sugars, 3g protein

Ingredients

4 frozen unsweetened peach slices, slightly thawed
¼ cup fat-free vanilla ice cream
2 ounces light vanilla soymilk
1½ ounces vanilla vodka
1 ounce sugar-free calorie-free peach-flavored syrup
¼ teaspoon lemon juice
⅔ cup crushed ice *or* 3 to 5 ice cubes

Directions

Place all ingredients in a blender, and blend at high speed until smooth.

Pour and enjoy. Peach-tastic!

MAKES 1 SERVING

Spiked Freckled Lemonade

PER SERVING (entire recipe, 1 drink): 122 calories, 0g fat, 60mg sodium, 4g carbs, 0.75g fiber, 2g sugars, 0g protein

Ingredients

Half a 2-serving packet (about ½ teaspoon) sugar-free
    lemonade powdered drink mix
8 ounces diet lemon-lime soda, chilled
1½ ounces vodka
1 no-calorie sweetener packet
4 frozen unsweetened strawberries, slightly thawed
⅔ cup crushed ice *or* 3 to 5 ice cubes

Directions

In a tall glass, combine powdered drink mix, soda, vodka, and sweetener. Stir until drink mix has dissolved. Pour mixture into a blender.

Add strawberries and ice, and blend at high speed until smooth. Pour into your glass and sip away!

MAKES 1 SERVING

Lava Smash

PER SERVING (½ of recipe, 1 drink): 177 calories, <0.5g fat, 42mg sodium, 19g carbs, 2g fiber, 10g sugars, 1.5g protein

Ingredients

For a pic of this recipe, see the photo insert. Yay!

3 ounces rum
8 frozen unsweetened strawberries, partially thawed
½ cup fat-free vanilla ice cream
4 ounces sugar-free calorie-free coconut-flavored syrup
¼ cup canned crushed pineapple packed in juice
2 no-calorie sweetener packets
1½ cups crushed ice *or* 8 to 12 ice cubes
Optional garnish: pineapple wedges

Directions

Add rum and strawberries to a blender and puree until smooth. Distribute evenly between 2 tall glasses.

Rinse blender. Place remaining ingredients in the blender, and add 4 ounces cold water. Blend at high speed until smooth.

Very slowly pour the contents of the blender over the strawberry mixture in the glasses. If you like, garnish each glass with a pineapple wedge. Enjoy!

MAKES 2 SERVINGS

Cocoa-nut Banana Rum-ble Frenzy

□▪

PER SERVING (entire recipe, 1 drink): 188 calories, <0.5g fat, 137mg sodium, 28g carbs, 2.5g fiber, 18g sugars, 2g protein

Ingredients

One 25-calorie packet diet hot cocoa mix
1 teaspoon fat-free non-dairy powdered creamer
1 no-calorie sweetener packet
1½ ounces coconut rum
Half a banana, sliced and frozen
¼ teaspoon coconut extract
1 cup crushed ice *or* 5 to 8 ice cubes

Directions

In a tall glass, combine cocoa mix, powdered creamer, and sweetener. Add 1 ounce hot water and stir until ingredients have dissolved. Add 2 ounces cold water and stir. Transfer to a blender.

Add rum, banana, coconut extract, and ice to the blender. Blend at medium speed until completely mixed.

Pour into your glass and enjoy!

MAKES 1 SERVING

For more recipes, tips & tricks, food finds, and MORE, sign up for FREE daily emails at hungry-girl.com!

Spiked & Slurpable Banana Split

◻◼◻◻◼◻◻◻◼◻◻◼◻◼◻◻◼◻◻◼◻◼◻◻◼◻◻◼◻◻◼◻◼◻◼

PER SERVING (entire recipe, 1 drink): 243 calories, 2g fat, 75mg sodium, 29.5g carbs, 3g fiber, 17g sugars, 3.5g protein

Ingredients

1 teaspoon Coffee-mate Sugar Free French Vanilla
  powdered creamer
4 ounces light vanilla soymilk
2 no-calorie sweetener packets
Half a banana, sliced and frozen
3 frozen unsweetened strawberries, slightly thawed
1½ ounces rum
1 cup crushed ice *or* 5 to 8 ice cubes
2 tablespoons Fat Free Reddi-wip
1 tablespoon light chocolate syrup
Optional garnish: maraschino cherry

Directions

Combine creamer with ½ ounce hot water in a glass, and stir to dissolve.

Add soymilk and sweetener. Stir and then transfer to a blender.

Add banana, strawberries, rum, and ice to the blender. Blend at high speed until completely smooth.

Pour into a tall (and possibly fancy) glass, and top with Reddi-wip, chocolate syrup and, if you like, a cherry. Dessert and a drink, all in one. WOOHOO!

MAKES 1 SERVING

Blendy Bananas Foster

PER SERVING (entire recipe, 1 drink): 227 calories, 2g fat, 89mg sodium, 25.5g carbs, 2g fiber, 15g sugars, 4g protein

Ingredients

 For a pic of this recipe, see the photo insert. Yay!

1 teaspoon Coffee-mate Sugar Free French Vanilla powdered creamer
4 ounces light vanilla soymilk
Half a banana, sliced and frozen
1½ ounces dark spiced rum
1 ounce sugar-free calorie-free caramel-flavored syrup
1 cup crushed ice *or* 5 to 8 ice cubes
2 tablespoons Fat Free Reddi-wip
½ tablespoon fat-free or light caramel dip, room temperature, stirred to soften

Directions

In a glass, combine creamer with ½ ounce hot water and stir to dissolve. Add soymilk and stir. Transfer to a blender.

Add banana, rum, syrup, and ice to the blender. Blend at high speed until smooth.

Pour into a tall glass, top with Reddi-wip, and drizzle caramel over the top. Indulge!

MAKES 1 SERVING

For Weight Watchers *POINTS*® values and photos of all the recipes in this book, check out hungry-girl.com/book.

Peach Melba
Daiquiri Slushie

Ingredients

1½ ounces rum
½ cup frozen unsweetened peach slices, slightly thawed
1 ounce sugar-free calorie-free raspberry-flavored syrup
2 no-calorie sweetener packets
¾ cup crushed ice *or* 4 to 6 ice cubes

Directions

Place all ingredients in a blender. Blend at high speed until thoroughly mixed.

Pour and enjoy!

MAKES 1 SERVING

Piña Colada Freeze

Ingredients

 For a pic of this recipe, see the photo insert. Yay!

1½ ounces coconut rum
1½ ounces sugar-free calorie-free
    coconut-flavored syrup
¼ cup fat-free vanilla ice cream
1 tablespoon canned crushed pineapple packed in juice
1 no-calorie sweetener packet
1 cup crushed ice *or* 5 to 8 ice cubes
Optional garnish: pineapple wedge

Directions

Place all ingredients in a blender, and blend at high speed until smooth
and completely mixed. Pour, garnish with a pineapple wedge (or not),
and enjoy!

MAKES 1 SERVING

Slammin' Slimmed-Down Strawberry Daiquiri

□■□■□■□■□■□■□■□■□■□■□■□■□■□■□■□■□■□■

PER SERVING (entire recipe, 1 daiquiri): 121 calories, 0g fat, 10mg sodium, 4g carbs, 0.5g fiber, 2g sugars, 0g protein

Ingredients

One 2-serving packet (about 1 teaspoon) sugar-free strawberry powdered drink mix
1½ ounces rum
3 frozen unsweetened strawberries, slightly thawed
½ ounce lime juice
1 cup crushed ice *or* 5 to 8 ice cubes

Directions

Combine drink mix with 4 ounces cold water in a glass and stir to dissolve. Transfer to a blender.

Add all other ingredients to the blender, and blend at high speed until slushy and uniform.

Pour, add a straw, and slurp that baby up!

MAKES 1 SERVING

HG Tip!

Feel free to experiment with whatever strawberry-blend drink mixes you find on shelves. Strawberry kiwi, strawberry banana, strawberry tangerine . . .

Watermelon Frojito

PER SERVING (entire recipe, 1 drink): 154 calories, <0.5g fat, 3mg sodium, 15.5g carbs, 1.5g fiber, 8g sugars, 1g protein

Ingredients

3 to 4 mint leaves
1 lime, cut into 4 wedges
2 no-calorie sweetener packets
¾ cup watermelon chunks, seedless or
    seeds removed
1½ ounces rum
1 cup crushed ice *or* 5 to 8 ice cubes

O◄ For a pic of
this recipe, see the
photo insert. Yay!

Directions

Place mint leaves, 2 lime wedges, and sweetener in a tall glass. Squeeze the juice from the remaining lime wedges into the glass and discard those wedges. Crush and muddle the contents of the glass. Set aside.

Place the watermelon, rum, and ice in a blender, and blend at high speed until smooth. Pour into the glass with the mint-lime mixture and stir well. Drink up and be refreshed!

MAKES 1 SERVING

Chilly Chocolate Mudslide

○■○■○■○■○■○■○■○■○■○■○■○■○■○■○■○■○■

PER SERVING (entire recipe, 1 mudslide): 156 calories, 0.5g fat, 177mg sodium, 10g carbs, 1.25g fiber, 6g sugars, 3g protein

Ingredients

One 25-calorie packet diet hot cocoa mix
2 no-calorie sweetener packets
2 ounces light vanilla soymilk
1½ ounces vodka
½ ounce sugar-free calorie-free white-chocolate-flavored
    or vanilla-flavored syrup
1 teaspoon light chocolate syrup
1 cup crushed ice *or* 5 to 8 ice cubes
Optional topping: Fat Free Reddi-wip

Directions

In a glass, combine cocoa mix with 2 ounces hot water. Stir to dissolve. Add sweetener and 1 ounce cold water. Stir and then transfer to a blender.

Add all other ingredients to the blender, and blend at high speed until mixed and delicious-looking.

Pour and, if you like, top with a squirt of Fat Free Reddi-wip!

MAKES 1 SERVING

Frozen Fudge-Dipped Strawberry Mudslide

PER SERVING (entire recipe, 1 mudslide): 193 calories, 1.5g fat, 94mg sodium, 20.5g carbs, 3g fiber, 4.5g sugars, 3.5g protein

Ingredients

 For a pic of this recipe, see the photo insert. Yay!

1 No Sugar Added Fudgsicle (or another frozen chocolate pop with about 40 calories)
2 ounces light vanilla soymilk
1½ ounces vodka
½ ounce sugar-free calorie-free strawberry-flavored syrup
3 frozen strawberries, slightly thawed
1 tablespoon sugar-free chocolate syrup
2 no-calorie sweetener packets
¾ cup crushed ice *or* 4 to 6 ice cubes
Optional topping: Fat Free Reddi-wip

Directions

Remove fudge pop from the wooden stick and place it in a blender. Add all other ingredients as well as 1 ounce water.

Blend at high speed until thoroughly mixed. For a thinner consistency, add another ½ ounce to 1 ounce water.

Pour and, if you like, top with Fat Free Reddi-wip!

MAKES 1 SERVING

For Weight Watchers *POINTS*® values and photos of all the recipes in this book, check out hungry-girl.com/book.

Spiked Pumpkin-licious Nog

Ingredients

40 ounces (5 cups) light vanilla soymilk
5 ounces rum
1 small (4-serving) package Jell-O Sugar Free
    Fat Free Vanilla Instant pudding mix
6 no-calorie sweetener packets
⅔ cup canned pure pumpkin
½ teaspoon ground nutmeg
½ teaspoon pumpkin pie spice
¼ teaspoon cinnamon
Optional topping: additional
    cinnamon

Directions

In a blender, combine all ingredients and blend at high speed until mixed thoroughly. Cover and refrigerate for at least 2 hours to allow it to thicken.

If you like, top each glass off with a sprinkling of cinnamon. Enjoy!

MAKES 5 SERVINGS

For more recipes, tips & tricks, food finds, and MORE, sign up for FREE daily emails at hungry-girl.com!

Chapter Four

Cool Classics

Yeah, these drinks are classics that HAD to be included.

There are some straight-up old favorites and some that have a new twist. Any way you *slurp* it, they're AWESOME and worthy of being served at ANY cocktail event or get-together. So start mixing!

My Oh Mai Tai

PER SERVING (entire recipe, 1 drink): 133 calories, 0g fat, 18mg sodium, 9g carbs, 0g fiber, 7g sugars, 0g protein

Ingredients

2 ounces diet lemon-lime soda
2 ounces pineapple-orange juice
1 ounce rum
3 drops almond extract
1 no-calorie sweetener packet
½ ounce dark spiced rum
Optional garnish: pineapple wedge

Directions

Combine all ingredients except dark spiced rum, mix well, and serve over ice.

Top with dark spiced rum. Garnish with a pineapple wedge (or not) and enjoy!

MAKES 1 SERVING

Bahama-rama

■□■□■□■□■□■□■□■□■□■□■□■□■□■

Ingredients

Half a 2-serving packet (about ½ teaspoon)
    sugar-free orange powdered drink mix
1½ ounces coconut rum
1 ounce pineapple juice
1 no-calorie sweetener packet

Directions

Combine powdered drink mix with 4 ounces cold water in a glass
and stir to dissolve.

Add all other ingredients and mix it up. Add lots of ice cubes and
then enjoy!

MAKES 1 SERVING

Wicked Good
White Russian

□ ◾ ◯ ◾ ◯ ▪ ◯ ◾ ◯ ▪ ◯ ◾ ◾ ◯ ▪ ◯ ◾ ◯ ▪ ◯ ◾ ◯ ◾ ◾ ◯ ▪ ◯ ◾ ◯ ◾ ◾ ◯ ▪

PER SERVING (entire recipe, 1 drink): 132 calories, 2g fat,
42mg sodium, 3g carbs, 0g fiber, 1g sugars, 1g protein

Ingredients

2 teaspoons Coffee-mate Sugar Free
   French Vanilla powdered creamer
1 teaspoon instant coffee granules
1½ ounces light vanilla soymilk
1½ ounces vodka
2 teaspoons sugar-free calorie-free
   vanilla-flavored syrup

Directions

In a glass, combine creamer and coffee granules with 2 ounces warm
water, and stir to dissolve.

Add soymilk, vodka, and syrup, and then stir it up.

Add many ice cubes and enjoy!

MAKES 1 SERVING

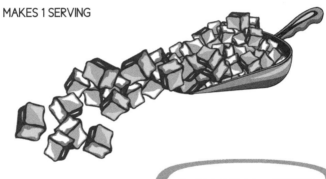

For Weight Watchers *POINTS*®
values and photos of all the
recipes in this book, check out
hungry-girl.com/book.

Blazin' Bloody Mary

PER SERVING (entire recipe, 1 drink): 126 calories, 0g fat,
413mg sodium, 6g carbs, 1g fiber, 4g sugars, 1g protein

Ingredients

4 ounces V8 Spicy Hot Vegetable Juice
1½ ounces vodka
2 teaspoons lemon juice
¼ teaspoon Worcestershire sauce, or
    more to taste
Dash salt, or more to taste
Dash black pepper, or more to taste
Optional: hot sauce (we like Frank's RedHot
    Original Cayenne Pepper Sauce)
Optional garnishes: celery stick, lemon wedge

Directions

Combine all ingredients and mix well. Serve over ice.

If you like it really spicy, add a dash of hot sauce. Garnish with the celery stick and the lemon wedge, if you like. Enjoy!

MAKES 1 SERVING

Mojito Madness

Ingredients

12 mint leaves
1 lime, cut into 4 wedges
1 cup crushed ice *or* 5 to 8 ice cubes
6 ounces diet lemon–lime soda
1½ ounces rum
Optional garnish: additional mint leaves

Directions

Place the mint leaves and 3 lime wedges in a glass. Muddle (a.k.a. pulverize). Top with ice.

Add the soda and rum, and stir well. Feel free to garnish with remaining lime wedge and extra mint. Feel very free to enjoy!

MAKES 1 SERVING

Hungry, Hungry Hurricane

PER SERVING (entire recipe, 1 drink): 132 calories, 0g fat, 15mg sodium, 7g carbs, 0g fiber, 7g sugars, 0g protein

Ingredients

½ teaspoon sugar-free orange-pineapple
  powdered drink mix
1 ounce passion fruit rum
1 ounce dark spiced rum
1 ounce sugar-free calorie-free
  black-cherry-flavored syrup
¼ teaspoon almond extract

Directions

Combine powdered drink mix with 4 ounces cold water in a glass and stir to dissolve.

Add all other ingredients and mix well. Toss in several ice cubes and get sipping!

MAKES 1 SERVING

Super-Sour Lemon Drop

□■□■□■□■□■□■□■□■□■□■□■□■□■□■□■□■□■□■□■

PER SERVING (entire recipe, 1 drink): 122 calories, 0g fat,
10mg sodium, 7g carbs, <0.5g fiber, 1.5g sugars, <0.5g protein

Ingredients

2 ounces fresh-squeezed lemon juice
1½ ounces vodka
2 no-calorie sweetener packets
4 ounces diet lemon-lime soda
Optional garnish: lemon wedge

Directions

Combine all ingredients except soda in a shaker filled with ice. Shake vigorously and strain into a glass.

Top with soda and give it a stir. Garnish with a lemon wedge, if you like, and drink up!

MAKES 1 SERVING

Kickin'
Cranberry Cosmo

PER SERVING (entire recipe, 1 drink): 100 calories, 0g fat, 32mg sodium, 2g carbs, 0g fiber, 1g sugars, 0g protein

Ingredients

5 ounces diet cranberry juice drink
1½ ounces vodka
1 teaspoon lime juice
Optional: splash of diet lemon-lime soda
Optional garnish: lime slice

Directions

In a shaker filled with ice, combine juice drink, vodka, and lime juice. Shake it up and then strain into a large martini glass.

If you like, top with a splash of soda and garnish with a slice of lime. Enjoy!

MAKES 1 SERVING

Upside-Down Tequila Sunrise

PER SERVING (entire recipe, 1 drink): 134 calories, 0g fat, 10mg sodium, 10g carbs, 0g fiber, 7.5g sugars, 0g protein

Ingredients

6 ounces light orange juice drink
1½ ounces tequila
1 teaspoon sugar-free calorie-free
    raspberry-flavored syrup

 For a pic of this recipe, see the photo insert. Yay!

Directions

Pour juice drink and tequila into a glass filled halfway with ice. Stir to mix.

Add syrup and gently swirl. Sip and smile (just not at the same time, or your drink will dribble down your chin)!

MAKES 1 SERVING

Bella Bella Bellini

┌───┐
│ PER SERVING (½ of recipe, 1 drink): 94 calories, 0g fat, │
│ 1mg sodium, 4.5g carbs, <0.5g fiber, 3g sugars, <0.5g protein │
└───┘

Ingredients

3 slices canned peaches packed in juice
One-fourth of a 2-serving packet (about ¼ teaspoon) sugar-free
    raspberry powdered drink mix
8 ounces sparkling white wine, chilled

Directions

On a small plate, mash peaches with a fork. Evenly distribute the
peach puree between two champagne flutes.

In a glass, combine powdered drink mix with wine and gently stir to
dissolve. Pour over the puree in the flutes and enjoy!

MAKES 2 SERVINGS

Chapter Five

Crazy-Good Crowd-Pleasers

This may be the most creative chapter in the book.

There are some standard party favorites—like sangria—but this chapter is also home to some of the most FUN cocktail-party creations we have ever dreamed up. Most notably, the Black Forest Jell-O Shot Desserts and both pudding-shot recipes. AAAHHHHHH, the pudding treats are so amazing, they inspired an HG Haiku . . .

Cocktail pudding fun,
Where have you been all my life?
Slurp or spoon—you choose!

By the way, pitcher drinks = your new BFF. Why? Making a big batch of drinks for a party ahead of time ensures that YOU don't get stuck mixing beverages to order all day/night and that you get to have fun with your friends. (That's the reason you have a party to begin with.) Yay!

Party-in-a-Pitcher Sangria

PER SERVING (1 generous cup): 125 calories, 0g fat, 5mg sodium, 13g carbs, 1.5g fiber, 7g sugars, 0.5g protein

Ingredients

1 cup sliced strawberries
1 small orange, peeled, chopped, seeds removed
1 small apple (preferably Fuji), chopped
Half a slightly under-ripe banana, peeled, chopped
½ cup canned pineapple chunks packed in juice, drained
One 750-milliliter bottle red wine
8 ounces diet cranberry juice drink
12 ounces diet lemon-lime soda

Directions

Place all fruit in a large container that will not stain easily, such as a glass pitcher or a high-quality plastic one. Add wine and juice drink, and give mixture a good stir.

Cover and refrigerate for at least 5 hours. (Overnight is best.)

Once ready to serve, stir in soda. Pour and be sure to get a nice amount of fruit in each glass. Enjoy!

MAKES 7 SERVINGS

HG Tip!

If you like your sangria with less alcohol per glass, add more of the cranberry juice drink until it tastes juuuuuust right.

Passion Fruit Orange Jell-O Shots

PER SERVING (1 Jell-O shot): 68 calories, 0g fat, 32mg sodium, 7g carbs, 0g fiber, 7g sugars, 0.5g protein

Ingredients

1 small (4-serving) package Jell-O Sugar Free
   Orange gelatin dessert mix
8 ounces passion fruit rum, chilled

Directions

In a large measuring glass or a mixing bowl, combine 8 ounces boiling water with gelatin mix. Stir until completely dissolved.

Add rum and stir again. Carefully pour the liquid into 8 small cups, about 2 ounces each.

Refrigerate for at least 4 hours, or until firm. Enjoy!

MAKES 8 SERVINGS

Mixed Berry Margarita, p. 34

Kickin' Key Lime Pie Martini, p. 10

Piña Colada Freeze, p. 51

Blendy Bananas Foster, p. 48

Lava Smash, p. 42

Winter Wonderland Peppermintini, p. 14

Watermelon Frojito, p. 54

HG's Magical Low-Calorie
Margarita, p. 28

Frozen Fudge-Dipped Strawberry Mudslide, p. 58

Upside-Down Tequila Sunrise, p. 76

Freezy Cocoa Puddin' Cups, p. 92

Swingin' Sangria, p. 88

Bacon-Bundled BBQ Shrimp, p. 144

Devilish Eggs, p. 118

Exploding Chicken Taquitos, p. 102

Sweet 'n Sassy Boneless Hot Wings, p. 124

De-Pudged Pigs in a Blanket, p. 96

Backyard BBQ Beef Cups, p. 140

Buff Chick Hot Wing Dip, p. 128

Mmmm-azing Mini Mushroom Tartlets, p. 114

Saucy Chick BBQ Nachos, p. 106

Red Hot Shots

Ingredients

One 750-milliliter bottle vanilla vodka
4 ounces sugar-free calorie-free
    brown-sugar-cinnamon-flavored syrup
¼ cup Red Hots Cinnamon Flavored Candy

Directions

Pour out 6 ounces vodka from the bottle, and reserve for another use.

Add syrup and candy to the bottle, replace the cap, and gently shake. Refrigerate overnight, or until candy has dissolved.

Shake and enjoy!

MAKES 15 SERVINGS

Sassy 'n Spiked
Pink Lemonade Pitcher

PER SERVING (1 generous cup): 110 calories, 0g fat, 67mg sodium, 3g carbs, 0g fiber, 1g sugars, 0g protein

Ingredients

48 ounces (6 cups) club soda
16 ounces (2 cups) diet cranberry juice drink
12 ounces (1½ cups) vodka
Two 2-serving packets (about 2 teaspoons) sugar-free
    pink lemonade powdered drink mix
8 no-calorie sweetener packets
3 lemons
Optional garnish: 8 additional lemon slices

Directions

Place all ingredients except lemons in a pitcher and stir well.

Cut lemons in half. Over a strainer, squeeze the juice into the pitcher.

Serve over ice and, if you like, garnish with lemon slices!

MAKES 8 SERVINGS

Tropical Vanilla Pudding Shots

Ingredients

4 ounces fat-free milk
1 small (4-serving) package Jell-O Sugar Free
    Fat Free Instant Vanilla pudding mix
3 ounces coconut rum
1 ounce lime juice
½ cup canned crushed pineapple packed in
    juice, not drained
1 cup Cool Whip Free, thawed

Directions

Combine milk and pudding mix in a bowl and whisk or mix until smooth. Add rum, lime juice, and pineapple, and stir well.

Fold in Cool Whip. Once mixture is smooth and uniform, divide it among 8 small cups.

Place in the fridge until ready to serve, at least 30 minutes. Enjoy with a spoon!

MAKES 8 SERVINGS

For more recipes, tips & tricks, food finds, and MORE, sign up for FREE daily emails at hungry-girl.com!

Swingin' Sangria

Ingredients

For a pic of this recipe, see the photo insert. Yay!

One 2-serving packet (about 1 teaspoon) sugar-free lemonade powdered drink mix
One 8-ounce can pineapple chunks packed in juice, not drained
2 cups sliced strawberries
1 orange, peeled, roughly chopped, seeds removed
1 peach or nectarine, roughly chopped
1 lime, sliced into rings
One 750-milliliter bottle pinot grigio
12 ounces diet lemon-lime soda

Directions

Combine powdered drink mix with 8 ounces water in a glass and stir to dissolve. Set aside.

Place all fruit in a large pitcher. Add lemonade mixture, 8 additional ounces water, and pinot grigio. Cover and refrigerate for at least 5 hours. (Overnight is best.)

Just prior to serving, stir in soda. Pour and be sure to get a nice amount of fruit in each glass. Enjoy!

MAKES 10 SERVINGS

For Weight Watchers *POINTS*® values and photos of all the recipes in this book, check out hungry-girl.com/book.

Black Forest
Jell-O Shot Desserts

□■

PER SERVING (1 dessert shot): 49 calories, 0.5g fat, 30mg sodium, 1.5g carbs, 0g fiber, 1g sugars, 0.5g protein

Ingredients

1 small (4-serving) package Jell-O Sugar Free
    Black Cherry gelatin dessert mix
4 ounces vodka, chilled
4 teaspoons mini semi-sweet chocolate chips
Optional topping: Fat Free Reddi-wip

Directions

In a large measuring glass or mixing bowl, combine 8 ounces boiling water with gelatin mix. Stir until completely dissolved.

Add vodka and 4 ounces cold water and stir again. Carefully pour the liquid into 8 small cups, about 2 ounces each. Refrigerate for 1 hour, until partially set.

Top each cup with ½ teaspoon chocolate chips. Refrigerate for at least 3 hours longer, or until firm.

Once ready to serve, top each serving with a squirt of Reddi-wip, if you like, and enjoy your dessert shot with a spoon!

MAKES 8 SERVINGS

Freezy Cocoa Puddin' Cups

PER SERVING (1 "puddin' cup"): 93 calories, <0.5g fat, 224mg sodium, 13.5g carbs, 0.5g fiber, 5.5g sugars, 1.5g protein

Ingredients

6 ounces fat-free milk
1 small (4-serving) package Jell-O
    Sugar Free Fat Free Instant
    Chocolate pudding mix
3 ounces coconut rum
1 cup Cool Whip Free, thawed
12 tablespoons Fat Free Reddi-wip

For a pic of this recipe, see the photo insert. Yay!

Directions

Combine milk and pudding mix in a bowl, and whisk or mix until thoroughly blended. Add rum and stir well.

Fold in Cool Whip. Once mixture is smooth and uniform, divide it among 6 small cups. Place in the freezer until mostly solid.

Once ready to serve, top each with a 2-tablespoon squirt of Reddi-wip. Enjoy with a spoon!

MAKES 6 SERVINGS

Chapter Six

Party Foods!

You can't have any sort of cocktail party, gathering, or girls-night-in get-together worth attending without snacks.

You know this. Here we're serving up 25 super-simple recipes for some of the world's most delicious guilt-free finger foods. Cheesy ones, crunchy ones, sweet ones, and spicy ones. What kind of kook wouldn't be interested in no-guilt pigs in a blanket, BBQ chicken nachos, pot stickers, tartlets, and potato skins?! Even if you don't DRINK, the recipes in this chapter ALONE make this book a great buy. So if you're reading this at the store, head to the register now!

De-Pudged
Pigs in a Blanket

PER SERVING (4 pigs in a blanket): 134 calories, 5g fat, 652mg sodium, 16g carbs, 0g fiber, 3g sugars, 8g protein

Ingredients

8 fat-free or nearly fat-free franks with about 45 calories each (like Hebrew National 97% Fat Free Beef Franks or Hoffy Extra Lean Beef Franks)
1 package Pillsbury Reduced Fat Crescent refrigerated dough

For a pic of this recipe, see the photo insert. Yay!

Directions

Preheat oven to 375 degrees.

Cut each hot dog into 4 even pieces. Set aside.

Take one of the eight triangle-shaped portions of the dough and stretch or roll it out slightly, making it into a larger triangle. Then, cut this piece of dough into four long, narrow triangles.

Beginning at the base of each of these triangles, roll one hot dog piece up in each until the point of the triangle wraps around the center. Place your blanketed pigs on a large, ungreased baking sheet. Repeat with remaining ingredients, so that you have 32 pigs in a blanket. Be sure to evenly space them, as the dough will expand while baking.

Place sheet in the oven, and cook for about 12 minutes, until dough appears slightly browned and crispy. Enjoy!

MAKES 8 SERVINGS

For more recipes, tips & tricks, food finds, and MORE, sign up for FREE daily emails at hungry-girl.com!

Super-Skinny Skins

□■

PER SERVING (4 pieces): 160 calories, 1g fat, 361mg sodium, 27.5g carbs, 4.5g fiber, 1g sugars, 10g protein

Ingredients

Three 8-ounce baking potatoes
½ cup shredded fat-free cheddar cheese
2 tablespoons precooked real crumbled bacon
Optional toppings: chopped scallions,
    fat-free sour cream, salsa

Directions

Preheat oven to 375 degrees.

Pierce potatoes several times with a fork, and place on a
microwave-safe plate. Microwave for 4 minutes.

Turn potatoes over, and microwave for 4 more minutes. Allow to
cool for a few minutes.

Cut potatoes in half lengthwise. Using a fork, gently scrape out the bulk of the flesh. Place the empty potato shells on a baking sheet sprayed with nonstick spray.

Bake in the oven for 8 to 10 minutes, depending on how crispy you like your potato skins. Then remove sheet from the oven, but leave the oven on.

Evenly distribute cheese and bacon among the potato skins. Return to the oven until cheese is hot.

Cut each potato skin in half. If you like, top with scallions, and serve with sour cream and/or salsa. Yum time!

MAKES 3 SERVINGS

Jalapeño Swappers

Ingredients

5 fresh whole jalapeño peppers
¼ cup fat-free cream cheese, room temperature
¼ cup shredded fat-free cheddar cheese
Salt, black pepper, and garlic powder, to taste
½ cup Fiber One bran cereal (original)
¼ cup fat-free liquid egg substitute
(like Egg Beaters Original)

Directions

Preheat oven to 350 degrees.

Halve the peppers lengthwise, and remove seeds, stems, etc. Wash
halves and dry them very well. Set aside.

Stir together cream cheese and shredded cheese. If you like, season with salt, black pepper, and/or garlic powder. Set aside.

Using a blender or food processor, grind Fiber One to a breadcrumb-like consistency. Season crumbs with salt, black pepper, and/or garlic powder. Place crumbs in one small dish and egg substitute in another.

Stuff pepper halves with cheese mixture. Carefully coat both sides of each pepper half, first with egg substitute, and then with Fiber One crumbs. Place peppers on a baking sheet sprayed with nonstick spray.

Bake in the oven for 25 minutes (for very spicy poppers) to 30 minutes (medium-hot poppers). Now eat!

MAKES 5 SERVINGS

HG Heads Up! Be VERY careful when handling jalapeño peppers. Wash hands frequently and well, and avoid touching your face and eyes.

Exploding Chicken Taquitos

○∎○∎○∎○∎○∎○∎○∎○∎○∎○∎○∎○∎○∎○∎○∎○∎○∎○∎

PER SERVING (2 taquitos): 197 calories, 2.5g fat, 594mg sodium, 22.5g carbs, 3g fiber, 2g sugars, 20.5g protein

Ingredients

 For a pic of this recipe, see the photo insert. Yay!

One 9.75-ounce (or 10-ounce) can 98%
    fat-free chunk white chicken breast
    in water, drained and flaked
½ cup salsa
⅓ cup shredded fat-free cheddar cheese
¼ teaspoon dry taco seasoning mix
Eight 6-inch yellow corn tortillas
Optional dips: red enchilada sauce,
    additional salsa, fat-free sour cream

Directions

Preheat oven to 375 degrees.

In a medium bowl, combine the chicken and salsa, and mix thoroughly. Cover and refrigerate for 15 minutes.

Remove chicken mixture from the fridge, and drain any excess liquid. Add cheese and taco seasoning, and mix to combine. This is your filling. Set aside.

Prepare a baking sheet by spraying it with nonstick spray. Set aside.

Dampen two paper towels, and place tortillas between them. Microwave for about 1 minute, until tortillas are warm and pliable. Take one tortilla (keep the rest between the paper towels), spray both sides lightly with nonstick spray, and lay it flat on a clean dry surface. Spoon about 2 heaping tablespoons of filling onto the tortilla. Spread it evenly across the entire surface, and roll tortilla up tightly, so that you have a cigar-shaped tube. Secure with toothpicks and place seam side down on the baking sheet. Repeat with remaining tortillas and filling.

Bake in the oven for 14 to 16 minutes, until crispy. Allow taquitos to cool for 5 minutes. If you like, dunk in enchilada sauce, salsa, or sour cream!

MAKES 4 SERVINGS

Sassy Veggie Egg Rolls

PER SERVING (2 pieces): 82 calories, <0.5g fat, 285mg sodium, 18g carbs, 1.5g fiber, 3g sugars, 3g protein

Ingredients

2½ cups dry cole slaw mix
1 cup chopped onion
½ cup chopped bean sprouts
½ cup chopped celery
½ cup canned pineapple packed in juice, drained and chopped
½ cup canned sliced water chestnuts, drained and chopped
¼ cup reduced-sodium/lite soy sauce
2 tablespoons chopped garlic
Salt and black pepper, to taste
12 large square egg roll wrappers (often stocked near the tofu in the fridge section of the market)

Directions

Preheat oven to 350 degrees.

Place slaw mix in a microwave-safe bowl with 2 tablespoons water. Cover and microwave for 3 minutes. Once cool enough to handle, drain water, and transfer to a large bowl.

Add all other ingredients except for wrappers to the bowl and mix well. Season to taste with salt and pepper. Set aside.

Place two egg roll wrappers on a clean, dry surface. Evenly place 2 heaping spoonfuls of the veggie mixture (1/12th of the total mixture) onto each wrapper, in rows a little below the center of each square. Moisten all four edges of each wrapper by dabbing your fingers in water and going over the edges smoothly.

Fold the sides of each wrapper about ¾ of an inch toward the middle, to keep the mixture from falling out of the sides. Then, roll the bottom of each wrapper up around the mixture, and continue rolling until you reach the top. Seal the outside edge once more with a dab of water.

Repeat process with all other wrappers, making sure you have a clean, dry surface each time. Place all of the egg rolls on a large baking sheet sprayed with nonstick spray. Lightly spray the tops of the egg rolls with nonstick spray.

Bake in the oven for about 25 minutes, until golden brown.

Allow to cool slightly, and then cut each egg roll in half. Party time!

MAKES 12 SERVINGS

Saucy Chick BBQ Nachos

□■□■□■□■□■□■□■□■□■□■□■□■□■□■□■□■□■□■□■

> **PER SERVING** (⅕th of recipe, about 14 loaded nachos): 229 calories, 3g fat, 875mg sodium, 26g carbs, 1.25g fiber, 7g sugars, 21g protein

Ingredients

4 ounces (about 70) baked tortilla chips
    (like the kind by Guiltless Gourmet)
One 9.75–ounce (or 10-ounce) can 98%
    fat–free chunk white chicken breast
    in water, drained and flaked
½ cup barbecue sauce with about
    45 calories per 2–tablespoon
    serving, divided
1 cup shredded fat–free cheddar cheese
2 tablespoons chopped scallions
Optional topping: fat–free sour cream

◯▪ For a pic of this recipe, see the photo insert. Yay!

Directions

Preheat oven to 350 degrees.

Spread out tortilla chips on a large ovenproof platter or baking sheet sprayed with nonstick spray. Set aside.

In a small bowl, combine chicken and ¼ cup barbecue sauce. Mix well, and then spoon mixture evenly over the chips.

Top evenly with cheese. Drizzle remaining ¼ cup barbecue sauce over the chips.

Bake in the oven for 8 to 10 minutes, until cheese and barbecue sauce are hot.

Sprinkle scallions over nachos. If you like, top or serve with sour cream. Enjoy!!!

MAKES 5 SERVINGS

Bacon 'n Cheese
Bell Pepper Skins

PER SERVING (2 pieces): 119 calories, 5.5g fat, 378mg sodium, 6.5g carbs, 1.25g fiber, 3.5g sugars, 11g protein

Ingredients

2 bell peppers (red, yellow, or orange)
6 slices extra-lean turkey bacon
¾ cup shredded reduced-fat cheddar cheese
¼ cup chopped scallions
¼ cup fat-free sour cream

Directions

Preheat oven to 350 degrees.

Cut peppers in half lengthwise. Remove stems and seeds. Slice each of those 4 pieces in half, leaving you with 8 slices, and set aside.

Spray a large baking sheet with nonstick spray. Place pepper slices on the sheet cut side up. Bake in the oven for about 20 minutes, until slices are soft.

Meanwhile, bring a large pan sprayed with nonstick spray to medium heat on the stove. Cook bacon on both sides until crispy. Let cool, and then chop into small pieces.

Once pepper slices are done, remove from the oven and let cool slightly. Don't turn off the oven.

Blot away any excess liquid from peppers. Sprinkle pepper slices evenly with cheese, scallions, and chopped bacon. Return to the oven and bake until cheese has melted, 5 to 10 minutes. Serve with sour cream and enjoy!

MAKES 4 SERVINGS

Oh My Squash!
Pot Stickers

□■□■□■□■□■□■□■□■□■□■□■□■□■□■□■□■□■

PER SERVING (5 pot stickers with sauce): 161 calories, 0.5g fat, 786mg sodium, 35g carbs, 3g fiber, 5g sugars, 4.5g protein

Ingredients

For Pot Stickers
3½ cups peeled and cubed butternut squash (about a pound)
½ cup grated carrots
¼ cup chopped scallions
2 tablespoons reduced-sodium/lite soy sauce
1 teaspoon chopped garlic
¼ teaspoon salt
⅛ teaspoon ground ginger
25 small square wonton wrappers (often stocked near the tofu in the fridge section of the market)

For Dipping Sauce
2 tablespoons reduced-sodium/lite soy sauce
1 tablespoon red wine vinegar
1 tablespoon sweet chili sauce

Directions

Place squash in a large microwave-safe bowl with ½ cup water. Cover and microwave for 12 to 14 minutes, until squash is soft.

Meanwhile, combine ingredients for dipping sauce in a small bowl, and refrigerate until you're ready to serve the pot stickers.

Once the bowl containing the squash is cool enough to handle, drain excess water. Using a fork or potato masher, mash squash completely. Add carrots, scallions, soy sauce, garlic, salt, and ginger, and mix thoroughly. This is your filling. Set aside.

Lay two wonton wrappers flat on a clean, dry surface. Spoon approximately 1 tablespoon of the filling into the center of each wrapper. Moisten all four edges of each wrapper by dabbing your fingers in water and going over the edges smoothly. Fold the bottom left corner of each wrapper to meet the top right corner, forming a triangle and enclosing the filling. Then press firmly on the edges to seal. Set aside, and repeat with all remaining wrappers and filling.

Once all wontons are assembled, bring a pan sprayed with nonstick spray to medium-high heat on the stove. Working in batches, cook wontons for 3 to 4 minutes on each side, beginning with the flat sides down, until crispy. (Between batches, remove pan from heat and re-spray with nonstick spray.)

Serve with dipping sauce and enjoy!

MAKES 5 SERVINGS

Pump-Up-the-Jam
Cocktail Weenies

PER SERVING (3 cocktail weenies with sauce): 75 calories, 1.5g fat, 619mg sodium, 12.5g carbs, 0g fiber, 3g sugars, 6g protein

Ingredients

1 cup chili sauce (the kind found by the ketchup)
¾ cup sugar-free grape or seedless blackberry jam
¾ cup very finely chopped onion
1½ teaspoons Dijon mustard
14 fat-free or nearly fat-free beef franks with
    about 45 calories each (like Hebrew National
    97% Fat Free Beef Franks or Hoffy Extra Lean
    Beef Franks)

Directions

Place all ingredients except franks in a crock pot. Stir until completely mixed.

Cut each frank into thirds, leaving you with cocktail-sized franks. Add those to the pot, and gently mix to coat.

Cover and cook on low for 3 to 4 hours.

Stir well and then serve up franks with extra sauce on top!

MAKES 14 SERVINGS

Mmmm–azing Mini Mushroom Tartlets

PER SERVING (5 tartlets): 120 calories, 5.25g fat, 260mg sodium, 14.5g carbs, 0.75g fiber, 1.5g sugars, 3.5g protein

Ingredients

 For a pic of this recipe, see the photo insert. Yay!

1 cup finely chopped portabella mushrooms
⅓ cup finely chopped white onion
3 tablespoons chopped scallions
3 tablespoons fat-free cream cheese, room temperature
½ teaspoon chopped garlic
⅛ teaspoon salt
2 dashes black pepper
2 dashes nutmeg
15 mini phyllo dough shells (found in the freezer aisle)

Directions

Preheat oven to 375 degrees.

Bring a pan sprayed with nonstick spray to medium-high heat on the stove. Add mushrooms and onion, and cook until soft.

Place mushrooms and onion in a small bowl. Add scallions, cream cheese, garlic, salt, pepper, and nutmeg, and mix well.

Evenly distribute mushroom mixture among the phyllo shells. Arrange shells on a baking sheet sprayed lightly with nonstick spray. Bake in the oven for 12 to 15 minutes, until edges of tartlets are crisp. Allow to cool slightly before serving. Yum!

MAKES 3 SERVINGS

Fruity Bruschetta

PER SERVING (2 pieces): 78 calories, 1.5g fat, 92mg sodium, 15g carbs, 1g fiber, 6.5g sugars, 1.5g protein

Ingredients

1 mango, diced
1 small banana, diced
½ cup diced strawberries
1 French baguette about 2 inches in thickness
    and at least 6 inches long
2 tablespoons light whipped butter or light
    buttery spread (like Brummel & Brown)
½ teaspoon cinnamon
2 no-calorie sweetener packets
⅓ cup fat-free fruit-flavored yogurt
    (your choice)

Directions

Preheat broiler.

Stir all fruit together in a bowl. Cover and refrigerate.

Using a sharp serrated knife, carefully cut sixteen ¼-inch-thick slices from the baguette. (Save any remaining bread for another use.) Lay bread slices in a single layer on a large baking sheet. Set aside.

Place butter in a small microwave-safe bowl and microwave until just melted. Add cinnamon and sweetener and mix well. Brush the tops of the bread slices with butter mixture.

Place the baking sheet about 5 inches beneath the broiler and let broil for 3 minutes, or until tops are slightly bubbly.

Evenly distribute chilled fruit among the bread slices. Top each with a teaspoon of yogurt.

Enjoy!

MAKES 8 SERVINGS

Devilish Eggs

Ingredients

[📷] For a pic of this recipe, see the photo insert. Yay!

2 cups roughly chopped orange cauliflower
¼ cup fat-free mayonnaise
3 wedges The Laughing Cow Light Original Swiss cheese
1 tablespoon sweet relish, patted dry to remove moisture
2 teaspoons minced shallots
1½ teaspoons yellow mustard
Salt and black pepper, to taste
10 hard-boiled eggs, chilled
Optional topping: paprika

Directions

Place cauliflower in a large microwave-safe bowl with ⅓ cup water. Cover and microwave for 6 to 8 minutes, until cauliflower is soft.

Once bowl is cool enough to handle, drain any excess water from cauliflower. Lightly mash cauliflower, and then place in a blender.

Add mayo and puree until just blended, not smooth. Do not over-blend.

In a mixing bowl, combine cauliflower mixture with cheese wedges, relish, shallots, and mustard. Stir until smooth.

Season mixture to taste with salt and pepper. Refrigerate for at least 1 hour.

When ready to serve, halve eggs lengthwise and remove yolks. Evenly distribute cauliflower mixture among egg white halves and, if you like, top with paprika.

MAKES 5 SERVINGS

HG Tip!

If you can't find orange cauliflower, use regular instead. But add a drop of yellow food coloring to the mixture if you want your Devilish Eggs to look like the real thing.

Sweet-Hot Steak Bites

PER SERVING (⅕th of recipe, about 6 "bites" with sauce):
196 calories, 4.5g fat, 254mg sodium, 18g carbs, 0.5g fiber,
15g sugars, 19.5g protein

Ingredients

One 8-ounce can crushed pineapple packed
    in juice, lightly drained
⅓ cup sweet Asian chili sauce
½ teaspoon reduced-sodium/lite soy sauce
¼ teaspoon crushed red pepper, or more to taste
1 pound raw lean beefsteak filet, cut into about
    30 bite-sized pieces
1 onion, finely chopped

Directions

Place pineapple, chili sauce, soy sauce, and crushed red pepper in
a crock pot. Mix well.

Add beef and onion and stir to coat.

Cover and cook on high for 3 to 4 hours or on low for 7 to 8 hours.

If you like, season to taste with additional crushed red pepper. Serve with excess sauce and toothpicks. Yum!

MAKES 5 SERVINGS

Mexican Bean & Cheese Dip

Ingredients

1 cup frozen ground-beef-style soy crumbles
   (like the kind by Morningstar Farms or Boca)
1 tablespoon taco sauce
¼ teaspoon dry taco seasoning mix
¼ cup fat-free cream cheese, room temperature
½ cup fat-free refried beans
½ cup canned black beans, drained
¼ cup chopped scallions
¼ cup canned diced tomatoes with green chilies, drained
¼ cup chopped fresh tomatoes
½ cup shredded fat-free cheddar cheese
Optional topping: fat-free sour cream

Directions

In a medium microwave-safe bowl, combine soy crumbles with taco sauce and taco seasoning. Mix well. Heat in the microwave for 30 seconds, and then set aside.

In a small dish, combine cream cheese with refried beans and mix well. Set aside.

Spray an 8-inch by 8-inch microwave-safe dish (glass is best) with nonstick spray. Layer the cheesy bean mixture on the bottom. Spread soy crumble mixture on top.

In another dish, combine black beans, scallions, canned tomatoes with chilies, and fresh tomatoes. Evenly spread this mixture in a layer on top of the "meat" mixture.

Sprinkle cheddar cheese over the entire dish. Loosely cover with microwave-safe plastic wrap.

Microwave for 5 minutes, or until cheese has melted. Top with sour cream, if you like, and serve with your favorite dippers!

MAKES 6 SERVINGS

Sweet 'n Sassy
Boneless Hot Wings

PER SERVING (4 wings): 134 calories, 0.75g fat, 387mg sodium, 15g carbs, 1g fiber, 7.5g sugars, 15.5g protein

Ingredients

For a pic of this recipe, see the photo insert. Yay!

8 ounces raw boneless skinless lean
   chicken breast, cut into 16 nuggets
¼ cup fat-free liquid egg substitute
   (like Egg Beaters Original)
¼ cup whole-wheat flour
2 dashes salt
2 dashes black pepper
¼ cup sweet Asian chili sauce
2 teaspoons seasoned rice vinegar
½ teaspoon crushed red pepper

Directions

Preheat oven to 375 degrees.

Spray a large baking sheet with nonstick spray and set aside.

Place chicken in a bowl, cover with egg substitute, and toss to coat. Set aside.

In a separate bowl, combine flour, salt, and black pepper, and mix well. One at a time, transfer chicken nuggets to the flour bowl, giving them a shake first to remove excess egg substitute—coat completely with flour, and then transfer to the baking sheet.

Bake in the oven for about 16 minutes, flipping halfway through, until chicken is fully cooked. Remove from the oven and set aside.

Combine chili sauce, vinegar, and crushed red pepper in a bowl and mix well. Add chicken and toss to coat. Now gobble up!

MAKES 4 SERVINGS

For Weight Watchers *POINTS*®
values and photos of all the
recipes in this book, check out
hungry-girl.com/book.

Crazy-Creamy
Spinach Artichoke Dip

Ingredients

One 8-ounce tub fat-free cream cheese, room temperature

¼ cup fat-free sour cream

¼ cup fat-free mayonnaise

¼ cup reduced-fat Parmesan-style grated topping, divided

¼ teaspoon salt

⅛ teaspoon cayenne pepper

3 tablespoons minced shallots

2 cloves garlic, minced

One 10-ounce package frozen chopped spinach, thawed
and drained thoroughly

One 14-ounce can artichoke hearts packed in water,
drained thoroughly and chopped

Half an 8-ounce can water chestnuts, drained and chopped

Directions

If you want to serve this dish hot, preheat oven to 350 degrees.

In a large bowl, combine cream cheese, sour cream, mayo, and 3 tablespoons Parm-style topping. Mix well. Add salt and cayenne pepper, and stir until smooth. Set aside.

In a pan sprayed with nonstick spray, cook shallots and garlic over medium heat on the stove until soft, 1 to 2 minutes.

Add shallot-garlic mixture to the large bowl, along with spinach, artichoke hearts, and water chestnuts. Stir well.

If serving dip cold, top with remaining 1 tablespoon Parm-style topping and you're done!

If serving dip hot, transfer to a medium casserole dish, top with remaining Parm-style topping, and then bake in the oven for about 30 minutes, until bubbly. Let cool slightly before serving.

MAKES 8 SERVINGS

Buff Chick Hot Wing Dip

.PER SERVING (about ¼th cup): 68 calories, 1.5g fat, 616mg sodium, 2g carbs, 0g fiber, 1g sugars, 10g protein

Ingredients

 For a pic of this recipe, see the photo insert. Yay!

One 8-ounce tub fat-free cream cheese, room temperature
½ cup Frank's RedHot Original Cayenne Pepper Sauce
½ cup shredded part-skim mozzarella cheese
¼ cup fat-free ranch dressing
¼ cup fat-free plain Greek yogurt (like Fage Total 0%)
Two 9.75-ounce (or 10-ounce) cans 98% fat-free chunk white chicken breast in water, drained and flaked

Directions

Place cream cheese in a large microwave-safe bowl and stir until smooth. Mix in Frank's RedHot, mozzarella cheese, ranch dressing, and yogurt.

Stir in chicken until thoroughly combined.

Microwave for 3 minutes. Stir and then microwave for an additional 2 minutes, or until hot.

Enjoy!

MAKES 15 SERVINGS

Yummy Yummy Eggplant Goo

Ingredients

1 medium-sized eggplant, peeled, cut into 1-inch cubes
1 red onion, chopped
½ red bell pepper, chopped
½ yellow bell pepper, chopped
¼ cup halved cherry tomatoes
1 tablespoon chopped garlic
½ tablespoon olive oil
1 teaspoon salt
¼ teaspoon black pepper
1 tablespoon tomato paste

Directions

Preheat oven to 400 degrees.

Arrange all vegetables in the bottom of a baking pan sprayed with nonstick spray. Sprinkle with garlic, olive oil, salt, and black pepper. Toss well.

Place pan in the oven, and roast for approximately 40 minutes, mixing occasionally, until vegetables are tender.

Once cool enough to handle, place the contents of the pan into a blender with the tomato paste. Pulse several times. Dip should be chunky, not smooth.

Proceed with dipping!

MAKES 8 SERVINGS

For more recipes, tips & tricks, food finds, and MORE, sign up for FREE daily emails at hungry-girl.com!

Sweet Caramelized Onion Dip

PER SERVING (⅓ʳᵈ cup): 74 calories, 1.75g fat, 512mg sodium, 11g carbs, 0.5g fiber, 4.5g sugars, 3.5g protein

Ingredients

1 tablespoon light whipped butter or light
    buttery spread (like Brummel & Brown)
2 large sweet onions, chopped
½ teaspoon salt
¼ teaspoon cayenne pepper
½ cup fat-free sour cream
½ cup fat-free mayonnaise
6 tablespoons fat-free cream cheese, room temperature
1 teaspoon Dijon mustard
1 teaspoon balsamic vinegar

Directions

Heat butter in a large pan over medium-high heat on the stove.
Once butter has coated the bottom of the pan, add onions,

salt, and cayenne pepper. Don't worry if onions are piled high in the pan—they will cook down.

Sauté for 10 minutes, stirring often. Reduce heat to medium–low, and cook for an additional 25 to 30 minutes, stirring occasionally, until onions are browned and caramelized.

Meanwhile, in a large bowl, combine sour cream, mayo, and cream cheese. Whisk until smooth, and then refrigerate.

Once onions are caramelized, add mustard and vinegar to the pan. Continue to cook for 5 minutes, stirring frequently. Remove onions from heat and allow to cool.

Once cool, add onions to the large bowl and mix dip thoroughly. Refrigerate overnight to allow flavors to combine. Serve at room temperature.

MAKES 6 SERVINGS

Four-Cheese Stuffed-Silly Mushrooms

Ingredients

12 medium-large baby bella mushrooms (each about 2 inches wide)
½ cup finely chopped onion
2 tablespoons chopped garlic
½ cup fat-free ricotta cheese
¼ cup fat-free cream cheese, room temperature
¼ teaspoon nutmeg
¼ teaspoon salt
½ cup canned spinach, thoroughly drained and dried
2 tablespoons shredded fat-free mozzarella cheese
2 teaspoons reduced-fat Parmesan-style grated topping
1 teaspoon garlic powder

Directions

Preheat oven to 375 degrees.

Gently remove stems from mushrooms. Chop stems into small pieces and set aside.

With the rounded sides down, place mushroom caps on a large baking sheet sprayed lightly with nonstick spray. Bake in the oven for 12 to 14 minutes. (Afterward, do not turn oven off.)

Meanwhile, bring a pan sprayed with nonstick spray to medium heat on the stove. Add chopped mushroom stems, onion, and chopped garlic. Cook and stir until garlic is soft, about 3 minutes. Set aside.

Once mushroom caps are cool enough to handle, pat dry until free of all excess moisture.

In a medium bowl, combine ricotta cheese, cream cheese, nutmeg, and salt until mixed well. Add mushroom–onion mixture, spinach, and mozzarella cheese. Stir until blended.

Evenly distribute cheese–veggie mixture among mushroom caps. They will be super–stuffed and the mixture will be piled on top, too!

In a bowl, mix Parm–style topping with garlic powder. Sprinkle stuffed mushrooms with this mixture.

Bake stuffed mushrooms in the oven for 8 to 10 minutes, until topping begins to brown. Let cool slightly and enjoy!!!

MAKES 4 SERVINGS

Tomato Bacon Tarts

PER SERVING (1 tart): 104 calories, 5.25g fat, 409mg sodium, 12g carbs, <0.5g fiber, 3g sugars, 3.5g protein

Ingredients

8 slices center-cut bacon or turkey bacon
2 small tomatoes, deseeded, finely chopped, patted dry
1 small onion, finely chopped
¾ cup fat-free mayonnaise
1 teaspoon garlic powder
1 package Pillsbury Crescent Recipe Creations
    Seamless Dough Sheet
2 tablespoons reduced-fat Parmesan-style grated topping

Directions

Preheat oven to 375 degrees.

Spray a 12-cup muffin pan with nonstick spray and set aside.

Bring a large pan sprayed with nonstick spray to medium-high heat on the stove. Add bacon and cook until crispy. Remove from heat and let cool.

Add tomatoes, onion, mayo, and garlic powder to a bowl. Once cool enough to handle, chop bacon and add to the bowl as well. Mix thoroughly and set aside.

Roll dough out into a 12-inch by 9-inch rectangle. Using a knife or pizza cutter, cut into 12 squares.

Place each square of dough into a muffin cup, and press it into the bottom and up along the sides of the cup to form a little "dough cup" for the bacon mixture.

Evenly distribute mixture among the cups. Sprinkle ½ teaspoon grated topping over each cup.

Bake in the oven for about 12 minutes, until golden brown. Let cool slightly, and then enjoy!

MAKES 12 SERVINGS

Fiesta Bites

Ingredients

12 small square wonton wrappers (often stocked near
   the tofu in the fridge section of the market)
2 tablespoons taco sauce
1 tablespoon fat-free cream cheese, room temperature
1 teaspoon dry taco seasoning mix
One 9.75-ounce (or 10-ounce) can 98% fat-free chunk
   white chicken breast in water, drained and flaked
¼ cup canned black beans, drained and rinsed
¼ cup corn, thawed from frozen
¼ cup shredded fat-free cheddar cheese
1 plum tomato, chopped
Optional: salt and black pepper

Directions

Preheat oven to 350 degrees.

Spray a 12-cup muffin pan with nonstick spray. Place each wonton wrapper into a cup of the muffin pan, and press it into the bottom and sides.

Lightly spray wrappers with nonstick spray. Bake in the oven for about 4 minutes, until the corners begin to brown. Leaving the oven on, set muffin pan aside to cool.

Mix taco sauce, cream cheese, and taco seasoning together in a bowl. Add chicken and stir until coated. Add beans, corn, and cheddar cheese, and stir well. If you like, season to taste with salt and pepper.

Evenly distribute mixture into the wonton shells, about 2 tablespoons each. Return pan to the oven and bake for about 8 minutes, until the chicken mixture is hot.

Once cool enough to handle, remove the filled wonton shells and top evenly with tomato. Serve and enjoy!

MAKES 12 SERVINGS

Backyard BBQ Beef Cups

PER SERVING (1 "beef cup"): 125 calories, 4g fat, 321mg sodium, 15g carbs, <0.5g fiber, 7g sugars, 7g protein

Ingredients

12 ounces raw extra-lean ground beef
1 small onion, finely chopped
¾ cup barbecue sauce
1 package Pillsbury Crescent Recipe
    Creations Seamless Dough Sheet

 For a pic of this recipe, see the photo insert. Yay!

Directions

Preheat oven to 375 degrees.

Spray a 12-cup muffin pan with nonstick spray and set aside.

Bring a large pan sprayed with nonstick spray to medium-high heat on the stove. Add beef and onion. Stirring frequently, cook until beef is crumbled and browned and onion is soft, about 8 to 10 minutes.

Reduce heat to low. Stir in barbecue sauce and let simmer for 5 minutes.

Roll dough out into a 12-inch by 9-inch rectangle. Using a knife or pizza cutter, cut into 12 squares.

Place each square into a muffin cup, and press it into the bottom and up along the sides to form a little "dough cup" for the beef.

Evenly distribute beef mixture among the cups. Bake in the oven for 12 to 15 minutes, until golden brown.

Let cool slightly, and then chow down!

MAKES 12 SERVINGS

For Weight Watchers *POINTS*® values and photos of all the recipes in this book, check out hungry-girl.com/book.

Good Chick Lollipops

□■

PER SERVING (2 "lollipops"): 196 calories, 3.5g fat, 315mg sodium, 10.5g carbs, 0.5g fiber, 0.5g sugars, 28g protein

Ingredients

12 ounces raw boneless skinless lean chicken breast, cut into 6 strips
1 ounce (about 15 pieces) Funyuns Onion Flavored Rings
½ ounce (about 7 chips) fat-free sour cream & onion potato chips
1 teaspoon onion powder, or more to taste
2 dashes garlic powder, or more to taste
2 dashes salt, or more to taste
⅛ teaspoon black pepper
2 tablespoons fat-free liquid egg substitute (like Egg Beaters Original)

Directions

Preheat oven to 375 degrees.

Carefully slide each chicken strip lengthwise onto a skewer. Set aside.

In a large sealable plastic bag, combine Funyuns, potato chips, and all the seasonings. If you like, add extra seasonings to taste. Seal the bag and crush contents until reduced to an almost breadcrumb-like consistency. Transfer to a plate and set aside.

Prepare a large baking sheet by spraying it with nonstick spray. Pour egg substitute into a small bowl.

Take a chicken skewer and dunk it in the egg substitute—use a spoon to evenly coat the chicken. Gently shake the skewer to remove any excess liquid, and then lay skewer in the seasoned crumbs. Rotate the skewer, pressing it into the crumbs, until it is evenly coated. Use your fingers or a spoon to add and pat crumbs onto any bare spots on the chicken. Transfer to the baking sheet, and repeat with all other chicken skewers.

Bake in the oven for 18 to 20 minutes, carefully flipping skewers about halfway through cooking, until chicken is cooked through and coating is crispy. Allow to cool for a few minutes, and then enjoy!

MAKES 3 SERVINGS

Bacon-Bundled
BBQ Shrimp

PER SERVING (4 pieces): 116 calories, 1.75g fat, 587mg sodium, 7g carbs, <0.5g fiber, 6g sugars, 16g protein

Ingredients

For a pic of this recipe, see the photo insert. Yay!

⅓ cup canned tomato sauce
3 tablespoons ketchup
1 tablespoon brown sugar (not packed)
1 tablespoon cider vinegar
½ teaspoon garlic powder
8 slices extra-lean turkey bacon,
     halved widthwise
16 large (not jumbo) raw shrimp, peeled,
     deveined, tails removed

Directions

Preheat oven to 425 degrees.

To make the sauce, combine tomato sauce, ketchup, sugar, vinegar, and garlic powder in a small bowl. Mix well and set aside.

Lightly spray a baking sheet with nonstick spray. Take a half-slice of bacon and coat it in the sauce. Wrap the sauce-covered bacon around a shrimp and place it, seam side down, on the baking sheet. Repeat with the rest of the bacon and shrimp. Give them a quick mist with nonstick spray.

Bake in the oven until shrimp are cooked through and bacon is crispy, 10 to 15 minutes. So good!

MAKES 4 SERVINGS

For more recipes, tips & tricks, food finds, and MORE, sign up for FREE daily emails at hungry-girl.com!

Okay, party animals, that's all we've got.
For now, anyway! Get more Hungry Girl
enjoyment by checking out the hundreds of
amazing recipes in our other books. And for
a daily dose of guilt-free tips, tricks, recipes,
food finds, and more, sign up for the free
daily emails at hungry-girl.com. *HG out!*

Index

notes

notes

notes

DON'T MISS THESE OTHER FABULOUS HUNGRY GIRL TITLES!

Hungry Girl:
*Recipes and Survival Strategies
for Guilt-Free Eating in the Real World*

Hungry Girl 200 Under 200:
200 Recipes Under 200 Calories

Hungry Girl 1-2-3:
The Easiest, Most Delicious,
Guilt-Free Recipes on the Planet

Hungry Girl Chew the Right Thing:
Supreme Makeovers for 50 Foods You Crave

Hungry Girl:
The Official Survival Guides:
Tips & Tricks for Guilt-Free Eating